Materials, Materials, Materials

Water

Chris Oxlade

Heinemann Library
Chicago, Illinois

Customer Service 888-454-2279

Visit our website at www.heinemannlibrary.com

Designed by Storeybooks
Originated by Ambassador Litho
Printed and bound in Hong Kong/China

06 05 04 03 02
10 9 8 7 6 5 4 3 2

Library of Congress Cataloging-in-Publication Data
Oxlade, Chris.
  Water / Chris Oxlade.
      p. cm. -- (Materials, materials, materials)
Includes bibliographical references (p.   ).
Summary: A simple presentation of information about water, including its composition, properties, and some of its uses.
  ISBN 1-58810-588-1 (lib. bdg.)   ISBN 1-4034-0089-X (pbk. bdg.)
  1. Water--Juvenile literature. [1. Water.] I. Title. II. Series.
  GB662.3 .O95 2001
  553.7--dc21
                              2001003929

Acknowledgments
The author and publishers are grateful to the following for permission to reproduce copyright material: p. 4 Sally Morgan/Ecoscene; p. 5 Karl Ammann/Ecoscene; pp. 6, 17, 19, 25 GSF Picture Library; pp. 7, 18 Tudor Photography; p. 8, 11 Corbis; p. 9 Anthea Beszant/Eye Ubiquitous; p. 10 Christine Osborne/Ecoscene; p. 12 Mike Maidment/Ecoscene; p. 13 Mike Whittle/Ecoscene; pp. 14, 20, 21 Chapel Studios; p. 15 Bennett Dean/Eye Ubiquitous; p. 16 Topham Picturepoint; p. 22 Mark Henley/Impact; p. 23 Stephen Rafferty/Eye Ubiquitous; p. 24 Still Pictures; p. 26 Hawkes/Ecoscene; p.27 Erik Schaffer/Ecoscene; p. 29 B&C Alexander/Still Pictures.

Cover photograph reproduced with permission of Corbis.

Every effort has been made to contact copyright holders of any material reproduced in this book. Any omissions will be rectified in subsequent printings if notice is given to the publisher.

Some words are shown in bold, **like this.** You can find out what they mean by looking in the glossary.

Contents

What Is Water?

Water is a **natural** material. Water is a **liquid.** It flows in streams and rivers. It fills the seas and oceans. The earth is covered with more water than land.

People need to drink water every day to stay alive. Every animal needs to drink water, too. Plants also need water to live.

Properties of Water

Rainwater is called **freshwater.**
So is water that comes out of the
faucets in your home. It has no
smell or taste. Water is also
transparent.

When you stir sugar into water, the sugar seems to disappear. This is called **dissolving.** Seawater has salt dissolved in it. That is why it tastes salty.

Ice and Steam

The water you drink is a **liquid.** But water can be a **solid,** too. Ice is solid water. Water turns to ice when it gets very cold. This is called freezing.

Water can also be a **gas.** Steam is water in gas form. Water turns to steam when it gets very hot. This is called boiling.

Clouds and Rain

Clouds are made of millions of very tiny drops of water. You can't see the drops when you look at a cloud, but they are there.

When the drops of water get big and heavy enough, they fall to the ground as rain. Some rain soaks into the ground. Some flows into streams and rivers and then back to the sea.

Finding Water

Some of the water we use comes from
reservoirs. A reservoir is made by
building a wall called a **dam** across
a river. The dam keeps the river water
from flowing away so we can use it.

There is water deep under the ground, too. To get to it, a hole called a well is dug into the ground. Then, water is pumped up from the bottom of the well.

Water to Your Home

Water flows to your home through
pipes. Big water pipes carry water under
roads and streets. Smaller pipes carry
the water to faucets in your home.

In many parts of the world, people do not have water in their homes. They often have to walk many miles to a well to get water.

Drinking Water

Your body needs water to work. People need to drink about a half gallon of water every day to stay healthy. That's the same amount as ten drink boxes!

Bottled water usually comes from a spring. A spring is a hole in the ground where water comes out. This water contains **chemicals** called minerals that are good for you.

Water for Plants

Plants need water to live and grow. They suck up water from the soil through their roots. Outside, plants get water from rain. You have to water plants that live indoors.

Some plants can live where it is very hot and dry. Cactus plants live in the desert, where it does not rain very often. To survive, they store water in their thick stems and branches.

Washing with Water

Water is good for washing things. This is because it picks up dirt and carries it away. Hot water washes things better than cold water.

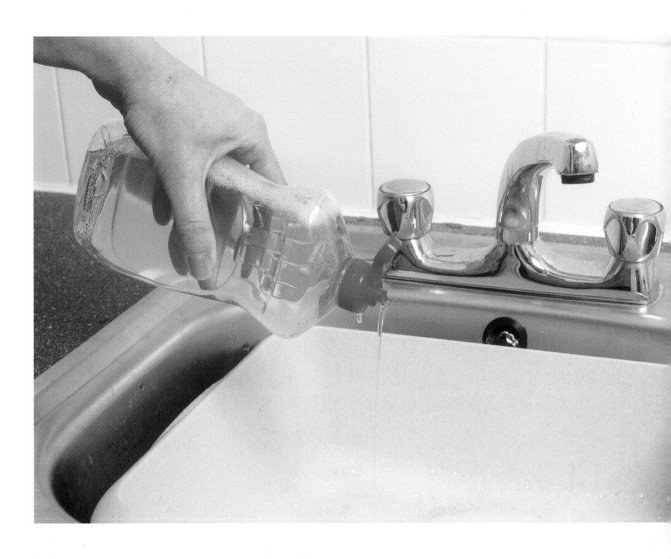

Water cannot wash away oil or grease by itself, though. You have to use soap, too. Soap breaks up the oil or grease and the water carries it away.

Water Power

We can use flowing water to make things work. At a water mill, rushing water from a river hits a big wheel. It makes the wheel turn. This makes machines inside the mill work.

Water is also used to make
electricity. Water is stored in a
huge **reservoir** behind this **dam.**
It rushes down big pipes and works
machines that make electricity.

Cleaning Water

Dirty water from homes and other buildings must be cleaned. It goes down a pipe from the sink or the toilet. Then it flows into a bigger pipe underground called a **sewer.**

The sewer carries the dirty water to a place where it is cleaned using special **chemicals.** Then, the clean water flows into a river or the ocean.

Water Pollution

In some places, people throw garbage into rivers and lakes, making them dirty. Harmful **chemicals** also flow in from **factories.** This is called **pollution.**

Sometimes dirty water from cities is not cleaned before it flows into the sea. This polluted water can make people and animals very sick.

Fact File

▶ Water is a **natural** material.

▶ **Freshwater** has no smell or taste.

▶ Seawater tastes salty.

▶ Water is **transparent.** You can see through it.

▶ The water you drink is a **liquid.**

▶ Water can also be a **solid,** called ice, and a **gas,** called steam.

▶ Water lets some **electricity** flow through it.

▶ Water is not attracted by **magnets.**

Can You Believe It?

There is a lot of ice frozen in the oceans. If all of it melted, the seas would rise enough to cover many islands and some cities near the coast!

Glossary

chemical   material used to clean or protect something

dam   strong wall built across a river to form a reservoir

dissolve   to mix together and disappear in a liquid

electricity   form of power that can light lamps, heat houses, and make things work

factory   big building where things are made using machines

freshwater   water that is clean and does not smell or taste like anything

gas   something that is invisible and does not have a shape, such as steam

liquid something that is wet and takes the shape of its container, such as water

magnet piece of iron or steel that pulls iron or steel things toward it

natural comes from plants, animals, or rocks in the earth

pollution harmful chemicals in the air, rivers, and seas

reservoir lake made by blocking water from a river

sewer big pipe that carries dirty water underground

solid something that has a size and a shape, such as an ice cube

transparent see-through

More Books to Read

Hewitt, Sally. *Water.* Danbury, Conn.: Children's Press, 2000.

Royston, Angela. *Solids, Liquids, and Gases.* Chicago: Heinemann Library, 2001.

Royston, Angela. *Water.* Chicago: Heinemann Library, 2001.

Williams, Brenda. *Water.* Austin, Tex.: Raintree Steck-Vaughn, 1999.

Index